LOST and FOUND

A SECOND GENERATION RESPONSE TO THE HOLOCAUST

LOST and FOUND

A POLISH EXPERIENCE

SOLLY KAPLINSKI

First published 1992

ISBN 0 620 16612 6

Typeset, printed and bound by Creda Press (Pty) Ltd, Cape Town

"Mine is yesterday, I know tomorrow"
Papyrus, Ptolemaic Dynasty

Solly Kaplinski's anthology is an important contribution to the literature on the Holocaust and serves to underline the living link from the past to the future through the present.

With the growing determination of revisionist "historians" to deny and re-write our tragic past, we, the second generation, are compelled to ensure that that "Experience" is never lost. We must not permit oblivion and the passing of time to defeat memory.

These writings of remembrance stand first and foremost under the sign of fidelity.

Solm Yach

ACKNOWLEDGEMENTS

To my wife, Arleen, for her friendship, unconditional love and wisdom.

To Solm Yach, man of vision, whose on-going support, encouragement and generosity turn dreams into reality.

To Ze'ev Mankowitz, mentor, role-model and friend.

To Liora Glazer, artist of understanding and sensitivity.

CONTENTS

PREFACE

My parents, who were constantly in danger and on the run when they were Partisans in the forests of Poland and Russia for five traumatic years, rarely spoke of their experiences or those of their families who were murdered by the Nazis. In an attempt to protect us, they seldom referred to the Holocaust, if at all, on the intellectual level. There was almost a sense of denial operating in our household.

Emotionally, of course, they carried the scars and were often prone to bouts of anxiety, panic and depression.

I, in my own way, tried to protect them and myself by avoiding references to their past; and in that sense I was an emotional cripple. My trip to Poland in April of 1988, however, as part of the "March of the Living" experience, was a cathartic moment for me: it released a gush of hitherto repressed and unabridged emotional responses (as reflected in these pages) and allowed me to express my mourning and come to terms with the death of my parents (*Zichronam Livracha*) both of whom passed away in 1987, within six months of each other.

It is to their memory that I dedicate this "stream of consciousness".

FOREWORD

Something mysterious happens when we stand with our dead in Poland. We immerse ourselves in destruction and emerge boiling with anger, yet committed to life. The enormity leaves us faint while we steel ourselves to prevent its recurrence. We hope that the concrete will make it more comprehensible, yet when we face the ruins of endless suffering we understand even less of it all. We know that these events unfolded fifty years ago but we respond as if it were yesterday. We step out of the onrush of events and find ourselves touching eternity; words and prayers that were once distant suddenly speak to us during *Minchah* in Auschwitz.

What draws us to Auschwitz is the nature of the deed and its chosen victims. "Why?" we ask and then again, "*Farwus*?" And the names on the suitcases tell us that there was system in the madness, a guiding principle. Those who worshipped death sought out those who celebrated life; those who sought to redeem the world through murder singled out those who believe that humankind will be redeemed in justice; those who saw human beings as beasts of the field sought to stamp out conscience and the image of God. That is why they created Auschwitz; that is why, in the final analysis, they sought to murder the People of the Book. In that valley of death we touch and are tested by the terrible mystery of Jewish existence.

Thus, even as we feel lost and are driven to silence, doors that were previously shut fast, open; almost unbidden we begin to speak and in speech we find our people, our parents, ourselves. We thank Solly Kaplinski, child of survivors, for allowing us to join his searing journey to the past.

Ze'ev Mankowitz

Dr Ze'ev Mankowitz is Senior Lecturer in Holocaust Studies at the Hebrew University School for Overseas Students in Jerusalem. He is also a lecturer at the Melton Centre for Jewish Education in the Diaspora.

He has been a visiting lecturer in Jewish History at Yale University, and a scholar-in-residence and educational consultant to numerous student, adult leadership and professorial groups in South Africa, Britain, America, Canada, Rumania, Austria, Poland and Israel.

He is currently Director of the Jerusalem Fellows — A Programme for Jewish Educational Leadership in the Diaspora.

11

Shylock:

". . . He hath disgrac'd me and hind'red me half a million; laugh'd at my losses, mock'd at my gains, scorned my nation, thwarted my bargains, cooled my friends, heated mine enemies. And what's his reason? I am a Jew. Hath not a Jew eyes? Hath not a Jew hands, organs, dimensions, senses, affections, passions, fed with the same food, hurt with the same weapons, subject to the same diseases, healed by the same means, warmed and cooled by the same winter and summer, as a Christian is? If you prick us, do we not bleed? If you tickle us, do we not laugh? If you poison us, do we not die? . . ."

W. Shakespeare
The Merchant of Venice
Act 3, Scene 1.

For Talya, Ronit and Carmi —
The Third Generation

THE ZHIDS ARE BACK!

I put on my Magén David[1] today
the first time since my Barmitzvah
in anticipation of a visit
to a
special
special place
the land of the anti-semites

I also wore my kippah[2] there
ahpikoris[3] that I sometimes am
to show off my Jewishness
(and my long nose)
to put the boot in
to be davka[4]

I didn't want
any misunderstanding
no subtlety
nor ambiguity
I wanted to drive the message home
loud and clear
forceably and with impunity:
Don't mess with us Jews
Ever.

I also wanted them to know
that us Zhids, Jewboys and Kikes[5]
we were back
in Poland
No — they didn't finish us off!

---

[1] Star of David; [2] skull-cap; [3] unbeliever
[4] contrary; [5] pejorative terms for Jews

14

Armed with our shofar[6] and the flag of Israel
one march
around Poland
was more than adequate.

---

[6] ram's horn sounded on the Jewish New Year and Day of Atonement
(used in commemoration of the sacrifice of Isaac). Also sounded in
battle in biblical times.

THE PARTY

In days gone by
the hosts threw a big party for their guests
Jews were on the menu
for
Hors-d'oeuvres
Main course
Dessert
and Coffee (black or white)
at
breakfast
lunch
and
suppertime

They, having eaten and disposed of
this sumptuous meal,
flushed the remains
down the toilet
into the bowels of the earth

The guests had a great appetite
and simply
couldn't get enough
The festivity carried on
till the early hours
of the
morning
right around the clock in fact

This popular party became a must
and everybody who was a nobody
got an invitation
(with an R.S.V.P.)
Sunday best was the suggested dress
on occasion

17

Rich food sometimes
wreaks vengeance on
gluttonous appetites
and causes considerable
discomfort and pain
doctors and dieticians tell us

So why couldn't these happy
and carefree
partygoers
choke on their vomit
a little sooner?

REQUIREMENTS FOR A FIRST-TIME VISITOR TO POLAND

Dictaphone
camera
sketch-book
and
diary

Gilbert's *Atlas*[1]
Wiesel's *Night*[2]

An open mind
a long concentration span
an obsession for detail
a capacity for grief

Instructions:

Capture the moment
hang on to every word
internalize the meaning
tell a friend
be a guardian of the past
revere our history

The Germans taught us all
about the value
of keeping records.

---

[1] Gilbert, M — *Atlas of the Holocaust*, London, 1982.
[2] Wiesel, E — *Night*, London, 1958.

19

THE CROSS OF POLAND

Everywhere you go
but especially
in the unpolished countryside
you see Mother Mary and Jesus
and the cross

It may've been my imagination
but as we drew nearer
the camps
so they seemed to proliferate
in abundance
especially the cross
placed strategically at the entrance of each home.

For what?
To ward off spirits?
To exorcise evil in the world?
To comfort their conscience?

The Polish pope continues
it seems
in the same vein
He embraces Kurt(z)[1] with it
props him up on it
(Haman[2] on a white horse?)
and so gives succour and nourishment
to other Jew-haters and murderers
and some Sunday-School 'teachers'

The crucifixion of the Jews continues.

---

[1] Play on Kurtz from Conrad's *Heart of Darkness* and Kurt Waldheim
[2] Grand Vizier to the ancient Persian king, Ahasuerus, who failed in his
attempt to massacre the Jews

STORY-TELLING IN THE SINGULAR

They say
it's all myth-making
After all
martyrs make for good heroes
and
nation building depends on mythology.

Heart-rending stories
tear-jerking tragedy
we all know
is the very stuff
of loyal adherents
and
rooted followers
and
passionate converts to the cause

O.K.
so let's pretend it wasn't
six million
say it was just
one murder
only
one gas chamber
just
one Adolf

I won't call you a liar and a cheat
if you say
it was
only one

How then do you expect me to respond?

It's still one too many.

IN THE SHOE SHOP

I went to a shoe shop
today
in
Majdanek
800 000 pairs on display
but
no
body
to fill them

How easy it must've been
to be ambitious
in
those days

It didn't take long
to fill a dead man's shoes.

LUBLIN — 4TH NOVEMBER 1943 — 10.30 A.M.

On 3 November 1943, 18 000 Jews were shot at Majdanek Concentration Camp. The camp is on the main Lublin road, less than three kilometres from the centre of the city, easy on the eye and within earshot. The S.S. called their day of slaughter the "harvest festival". (Gilbert's *Atlas of the Holocaust*, London 1982, page 174.)

I heard Carole King in Poland today
on the way back from Majdanek
'You've got a friend,' she sang on the radio
We were passing over Lublin at the time
— just three kilometres away

I pictured a Lublin shopping scene
the morning after
the day before:
the hustle and bustle of the C.B.D.
housewives at the market-place
looking for bargains
husbands drinking piping hot coffee
in the local café
engaged in earnest discussion

I wondered:
Could the topic of their conversation be:
the inclement weather?
cheating on their wives?

Did anyone dare ask:
Heard anything unusual yesterday?
Anything untoward?

How about the teachers?
How did they respond to their pupils —
they surely must've asked some questions
or did their parents persuade them otherwise?

I imagined some answers to
that unasked question:
a backfire of motor car engines
a cacophony of geese flying overhead
thunder and lightning

or how about this one:
a needle stuck in a groove of the 1812 overture?

Carole King returned soulfully to my thoughts
'When you're down and troubled and
need a helping hand . . .
You've got a friend.'

'What's three kilometres among friends?'
I cried to myself.

The shortest distance between two points is a life-line.

LUBLIN — 4TH NOVEMBER 1943 — 2.30 P.M.

They told us (they still do)
that they never
heard anything
saw anything
knew anything
okay — so let's give them the benefit of the doubt
for a moment
but just for a moment.

They can never say
they smelt nothing
Surely human flesh and bone
baking in those ovens
surely
battered bodies barbecued on pyres
must've aroused
some new sensations?

Let's make another assumption
for a moment
but just for a moment
that those who enjoy a hearty steak
can't tell the difference between man and beast
— even without seasoning

Okay
but how to explain away
the blanket of human ashes
so lovingly conveyed by the gentle breezes
on to the city?

They say the most popular item
in the store that day was soap —
Shades of Lady Macbeth?

The gardens in the Spring of '44
were the finest ever
rich, lush and an array of spangled colours
so many beautiful flowers in full bloom
and tantalising scents

The winter compost made a perfect fertilizer.

IT'S HARD TO BE HUMBLE

I saw many caps on display today
in the cap store
at Majdanek
all sorts and sizes
but especially
large, medium and small

Only one was missing —
swollen-headed

Can you blame us today
for being swollen-headed?

We are used to going cap in hand
We did it once too often
and
lost our heads.

THE TREES OF POLAND — A FAILED BLOOD TRANSFUSION

Ballet has a new meaning for me now:
the trees of Poland
somehow remind me of
ballet dancers
so elegant and graceful in repose.

Just think:
as saplings
they were suckled not on mother's milk,
the stuff of human kindness,
but on the
blood of my brothers
scattered all over
this accepting earth.

Pity these selfsame trees
can't give witness to
their experience
as saplings.

The young somehow always have
a clearer vision.

ACCOMMODATION FULLY BOOKED

When Auschwitz opened its well-oiled gates
to welcome weary and unsuspecting travellers
everyone, yes everyone
was blinded
by this new liberation theology

Promises of freedom (with fingers crossed)
seemed attractive and inviting
One couldn't help but
prolong one's stay
on a permanent basis

Pity there was no time-sharing then.

WITH JONNY AT AUSCHWITZ

'I feel so guilty,' Jonny said
with tears in his eyes
'I can't cry, nor despair
and yet
I see the death of
all my people
How do I grieve?
Why can't I break?
I so want to mourn.'

What could I
a child of
Buried Survivors
I who never feel a thing on Yom Hashoah[1]
(I lived it every day of my life)
say?

I said to him as best as I could
'Jonny, it's O.K.
You don't have to feel guilty
This is after all a museum
— it's even called one
You see everything is
neatly sheltered
and
Germ
ethodically
stacked
behind
glossy glass
preserved for posterity
at perfect room temperature.'

---

[1] The day dedicated to remembering the Holocaust

I wanted to say
'The only things missing in
this museum
are stuffed animals,'
but I thought it inappropriate
given the circumstances
you will agree.

And yet
I couldn't help thinking
that butchered bodies
shards of bone
even
créme
hate
d
ashes
would've lent an air of
authenticity
to the scene
Maybe that would've broken Jonny up.

Instead I, feeling inadequate (very)
put
my hand on his shoulder
and tried
to comfort him
and ease his guilt.

Knowing Jonny as I came to know him
I felt he didn't need to cry.

He doesn't need his tears
to record
our history.

A NEW THEORY OF MOTIVATION

Clearly
when they hacked off our hair
they thought
they'd stamp out our strength —
that didn't work
When they yanked out our teeth
they hoped
to silence us —
that didn't work
When they burnt our bodies
they assumed
we'd rest
in pieces
forever —
that didn't work
When they roasted our brains
they dreamed
of obliterating our past —
that didn't work
When they massacred our children
they expected
to blot out
our future —
that didn't work
When they torched our Torah
they planned
to annul
our mission —
that didn't work

Is it possible
that all along
they knew
it wouldn't work
that they really had
other things in mind
(in those innermost recesses)?
Was there
in other words
method in their madness?
(Freud would've had a field-day here.)

Is it
within the realm of possibility
that they really
wanted to speed up
the State of the Jews?

Did they take pity on us?
Is that it?!

The mind boggles . . .
Were they really Zionists at heart?!
Was this whole Judenrein[1] thing
part of a plot
an international conspiracy
to put us Jews
in our place?

The sheer genius of it!
'What a piece of work is a man!
How noble in reason!'[2]

---

[1] free of Jews (uncontaminated)
[2] W. Shakespeare, *Hamlet*, Act 2, Scene 2

40

They didn't really want
to take away
people's reason
for living.

That would have been the final solution.

THE ART OF PHOTOGRAPHY — OR IS IT A SCIENCE?

How do you photograph
a crematorium?

At what angle do you point your lens?

Do you shoot in Kodakolour
or black and white?

What about a
Flash of Light
to enhance quality and meaning?

Can the human eye really filter
the experience?

And even if the perfect picture emerges
so bloody what?

It's just another addition
to our over-stuffed photo album
of
   faded

      memories

JOB SATISFACTION

Urgent
Required A.S.A.P.
in the national interest
a gas chamber operator
preferably no qualifications or previous experience
(Ph.D also acceptable)

Generous working conditions (shift work)
pleasant company
bonuses and commission

Opportunities for expanding experience
and achievement
security of tenure
in a progressive organisation
with well-defined goals

Salary: negotiable

In-house training
minimal supervision thereafter
little initiative required
communication skills: not essential

Recommended:
A strong sense of patriotism
a calling
missionary zeal
single-mindedness

Additional details:
The chamber is easy to operate:
child's play
built to specification
compatible, convertible, adaptable
user-friendly
no memory.

A generous supply of software
is provided.

Note:
We anticipate an overwhelming response
and may not
be able to reply
to all applicants
individually.

Applications to include:
at least two testimonials
from significant members
of your community
e.g. minister, principal, mayor
plus
family tree.

An excellent career opportunity
for the right-minded candidate.

THE VALUE OF PRAYER

Mincha[1] in Auschwitz
was a routine affair
or so I thought

Barely a minyan[2]
and everyone
rushing through the
Amidah[3]
to beat the rain and bitter cold, the bitter cold

Our little prayer group
somehow attracted others
needing to find shelter
and warmth

Now, I'm not sure
if I'm a God-fearing man
or even
if I believe

But the intonation of those
Assembled Voices
the incantation of
'God's Chosen'
that Auschwitz congregation
of our people
brought me closer as never before

I now understand
a little better
the value of prayer.

---

[1] the afternoon prayer
[2] a quorum of ten males
[3] a standing prayer of silent devotion to God

שְׁמַע יִשְׂרָאֵל ה' אֱלֹהֵינוּ ה' אֶחָד

הֲשִׁיבָה שׁוֹפְטֵינוּ

וְהָסֵר מִמֶּנּוּ

לְבַדְּךָ בְּחֶסֶד וְרַחֲמִים

בָּרוּךְ אַתָּה ה'

וְיוֹעֲצֵינוּ כְּבַתְּחִלָּה וּמְלוֹךְ עָלֵינוּ אַתָּה ה' לְבַדְּךָ

מֶלֶךְ אוֹהֵב צְדָקָה

תִּתְקַדֵּשׁ כְּרָאוּתָהּ שְׁמָהּ רַבָּא

A FAMILY REUNION

Fancy meeting you here
Tamar
my long-lost cousin
In Auschwitz
of
all
Places

In the crematorium

In that very
place
where
families
were torn
a
　　part

butchered
and burnt

We, you and I,
came together and
locked in embrace
mutual love
and tears of unspeakable happiness.

SNOWFLAKES IN AUSCHWITZ

Gently, silently and quickly they came
in their millions
fluttering down
to join us
kissing our cheeks
warming our bodies
insulating us —
a pale duvét of down feathers
a column of white cloud
showing the way
to Bnei Yisrael[1]
in a man-made desert.

In that Galut[2] wasteland
where all our best dreams and ambitions
went up
in smoke
we
comforted by this presence
sustained by this manna
continued our march briskly
to the Promised Land.

---

[1] the children of Israel
[2] Exile

OLD MONEY

They're still playing our song
It may be in a
different key
cleverer improvisation
a little more up-market
But it's the same old tune:

There's no business like Jewbusiness
— it's the best show in town.

Torah scrolls, Shabbos[1] candles, Channukiyot[2] and
Seder plates[3]
'foon der heim'[4]
all proudly displayed
by puffed-up possessors
at flea-markets of all places
They line their pockets
with a piece of our past.

You want to pay for more relics
of way back when?
Nu?[5]
Take in the 'Yiddish' theatre
Shed a subsidized tear
for the old folk.

---

[1] Sabbath
[2] candle stick holder for eight candles; lit on Festival of Lights (Chan-
nukah) which marks the liberation of the Jews of Palestine from the
oppression of the Syrian-Greeks (165 B.C.E.)
[3] ceremonial plate used on Passover
[4] from the old country
[5] so

Judaics
POLAND

15 Złoty

1 Złoty

200 Złoty

But best of all
for the passing trade
those 'museums'
(replete with souvenir shops
and sweet things to eat)
with tourists by the airconditioned busload
(it used to be trucks and trains)
belched into those caverns of darkness.

Yes,
the Jews are back in Poland
again
in a big way —
a familiar refrain
a variation on a theme.

What a lesson for your
neighbourhood stockbroker!
What inspiration
for budding entrepreneurs!

Safeguard your future
'make a fence'
against inflation.

There could be no surer
long-term investment
than these
'footnotes of history'.

UNTITLED

Without warning
the wallet was gone
disappeared out of sight
not a trace
We searched high and low
retraced our steps
made frantic enquiries
all to no avail.

In a final act of revenge
nimble Polish fingers
in a lucky-charm shop
(Is it against Halacha[1] for Jews to have luck?)
removed the final piece of evidence
from my wife's bag:
a shakily scribbled Vilna address
(my mother's childhood home)
written by my father on his deathbed
(I didn't know then)
his very last words.

All thought of making it to Vilnius
(Must they bastardize the name as well
appropriate it
make it Judenrein?[2])
seemed pointless then.

I wonder
if that ganif[3]
can know of
Hitler's
posthumous
victory.

---

[1] Jewish Law; [2] free of Jews (uncontaminated); [3] thief

55

A PLEASURE TRIP — SO WHAT'S NEW?

Hey, all you jet-setters,
have you heard?
There's a new spot on the tourist agenda;
it's simply a must.

Come to Poland,
one and all,
and see
a cottage industry
of concentration camps.

But whatever you do
don't you forget
your designer clothes and stonewashed jeans
and especially your Rayban sunglasses;
make sure though
the shades aren't too dark —
your make-up won't show
(nor will your tears).

But the most important things to remember
are your traveller's cheques — American Express
bargains galore to be found in Poland
leather jackets from Paris
chocolates from Brussels
liquor from London —
all sold for a song.

You can indulge in your favourite pastime and hobby
even cut your trip short.
And what will you tell the folks back home
or your bosom buddies green with envy?

That the weather was fine
the talent was great
no McDonalds around but the food was okay
and as for the camps
they were simply stunning?

I feel for you descendants of the 13th tribe —
destined to be lost forever.

REAP WHAT YOU SOW

The best time to visit Treblinka
(the only time)
(and once only)
is after the rainy season.

Don't be deceived (at first) by
chirping birds
manicured lawns
and tall, handsome pines.

Don't be fooled by
the symbolic rock cemetery (official)
or the polished stone tomb.

Let the truth be told.
Let the horror unfold itself.
Let the facts cry out for themselves.

Treblinka is a massive graveyard
ahn oonglick[1].
(What are the limits for Cohanim[2]?
a shayla for the Rav[3])
As far as the naked eye can see
with each scoop of soil
under your feet
in the damp, dark, dank soil
an underworld emerges.

'Dem bones are gonna rise again . . .'
The Prophet never lies.

---

[1] a disaster, a catastrophe
[2] the high priests
[3] a question for the Rabbi

Treblinka soil yields
a bountiful crop
a rich harvest.

And they call the Israelis 'Nazis'!

TREBLINKA

RESPECTING THE PASSED — RITES FOR THE DEAD

I normally daven[1] mid-week
in a minyan[2] of mourners
True on Shabbat[3]
my shul[4] — like others
also has non-mourners
(a handful)
who come to be inspired
or-for-whatever reason.

I always used to
divide up
shul-goers into mourners and non-mourners,
But now
Kaddish[5]
in Auschwitz and Majdanek
reminds me
I have no right to appropriate mourning
for myself alone
no matter how painful
being an Avel[6] is.

In a nation of mourners
the chanting of Kaddish
is too sacred
to be confined
to the domain
of the personal
only.

After all,
Hitler went back
generations.

---

[1] pray; [2] a quorum of ten men; [3] the Sabbath
[4] synagogue; [5] the mourner's prayer; [6] mourner

JEWISH BOOKKEEPING

It's not enough that they
chopped out our hearts
spewed out our souls
and
took our breath away.

They also usurped our history
and
denied our past.

They didn't believe our Prophets;
now they think we hallucinate!

Let's give them
noughts
for their comfort.

THE READING OF THE WILL
(Some Thoughts at the Warsaw Jewish Cemetery)

Where was the vision?
the foresight?

You
people of culture and wealth
who made it to the very top
who perpetuated yourselves
in polished palatial tombs,

Where did it get you in the end?
broken matzevahs[1]
vandalised inscriptions
people pissing on your last resting-place.

This surely couldn't've been the plan —
to dig your own grave
and bury others?

What legacy did you leave behind
for your children and grandchildren?

Such scholars
Such Talmidei Chachamim[2]
Don't you ever learn from history?

Jews are often an idea
whose time has come
and then
they overstay their welcome.

---

[1] tombstones
[2] wise scholars

There's no one even left
to say Kaddish
for you.

ROLE MODEL

Being a Cohen
I was torn
I so wanted to explore the Warsaw Cemetery
but somehow
I held back
catching only glimpses
of those monumental mausoleums.

I wandered off the beaten track
and came upon Korczak's statue
a child wrapped in his arms
little ones trailing behind
I saw an old Jewish lady
place a single simple flower
on his stone.
Mit tzubrochena tzeina[1]
I tried to engage in conversation with her
but she (tears in her eyes)
was reluctant.
I wanted to ask:
did you know him?
perhaps you knew children in his care?
your child?
was he a family member?
what was he like?

Steve
my teacher
at the Hebrew University
kindled the interest
ignited the flame

---

[1] Yiddish for 'with broken teeth', i.e. speaking with considerable
difficulty

inspired me to read Korczak;
and the more I read the more I felt
the aura of a superman —
and yet
so humble, so understanding
of the frail human condition.

Tears welled in my eyes
as I looked again
at those puppy innocents following Janucz
hand-in-hand.
(Could they really have known?)
I wanted so desperately to be in that line
to walk in his footsteps
to be in his shadow.

The old Jewish lady (with the solitary flower)
embraced my sobs
sha sha'd[2] me down
until I was
at
peace.

In their presence
I no longer felt
an orphan.

---

[2] quietened

POLAND — SOME HOME TRUTHS

Clutching my Gilbert
close to my chest
I travelled through Poland
hoping to gain
a new understanding

His well-thumbed Atlas
(my Bible)
filled in some gaps
provided the detail
gave me fresh insights

posed many more questions.

I still could not fathom
the silence of my parents
why they rarely spoke about
It.

I'd always known
they were different from others.

The nightmares, the screams
the pain-filled recurring dreams
the fear of the doorbell
the panic at the shrill telephone ring
the never-ending paranoia and mistrust
the obsession with the ein hora[1]
could never quite cover up
the games they played
to over-protect my brother and me —
neither could their oft acted-out anxieties.

------

[1] the evil eye

And then one day
walking through a cast-off street
of Warsaw
seeing all those tell-tale signs
of once sturdy Mezuzot[2] on ancient door-frames
and feeling a bitter rage
at the gouging out
of the very heart of Judaism
in this now 'ghost city'
some truths
were revealed to me
about my home secrets.

What is there left to say
to innocent children
when the very centre of your gravity
has been cruelly dislodged
when you've been denuded and deflowered
and utterly robbed of all your dignity
and all that remains
is a permanent scar on the heart?

Isn't it easier to play make-believe?
and yet:
so many things
left unsaid
unexplained
unexpressed
unshared.

I couldn't even get a foot in the door.

---

[2] prayers from the Bible written on parchment, placed in a case and
attached to the doorpost

TO GO HOME?

I owe it to you Mom & Dad
even tho' you rest in the earth
to go home

I owe it to you my bobbas and zeidas[1]
whom I never knew
who could never spoil me
and who were shoved
alive
into a mass burial-pit
in the Ponary Forests
to go home

Home conjures up images of
warmth, familiar smells
laughter
security
and peace of mind

Poland may've been home then
but it's really hell on earth
It's evolution in reverse
It shakes you to your very core
It makes you fear for man

So why go back you may ask

To remember
to bear witness
to be the link
to pay homage
to take care of the past.

---

[1] grandmothers and grandfathers

EPILOGUE: THE BOTTOM LINE

How many times must we stand up for the rights of others?
We must — to the nth degree
and yes
let's proclaim it to the world
(they always want proof)
but it's still not enough.

How many injustices must we confront
on behalf of others?
We must — to the nth degree
and
let's shout it from the barricades
but it's still not enough.

How many banners must we hold up
and how many miles must we march
for the dignity of others?
We must — to the nth degree
but it's still not enough.

They know
yes they do
when the crunch comes
we always stand up
to be counted
but it's still not enough.

So let me ask you
very tentatively
with tears in my eyes
will it be enough only
when we turn the other cheek?

בְּכָל־דּוֹר וָדוֹר חַיָּב אָדָם לִרְאוֹת אֶת־
עַצְמוֹ, כְּאִלּוּ הוּא יָצָא מִמִּצְרָיִם

"In each generation, every person should feel as though he or she has actually been liberated from Egypt."

The Passover Haggadah

Reader's Response

The author invites comments from the reading public (to be addressed to him at P.O. Box 3508, Cape Town 8000, Republic of South Africa).